Fergus McGonig … Laureate,
former teacher, … musician
(although at no s … mer poet).
He lives in Birmir … a recently
fitted revolving … collection
of poetry.

Send More Pianos

Fergus McGonigal

Bx3

This edition published by Bx3, an imprint of Burning Eye Books 2019

www.burningeye.co.uk

@burningeyebooks

Burning Eye Books
15 West Hill, Portishead, BS20 6LG

ISBN 978-1-911570-99-8

For Jon Bowen.
In the absence of more pianos,
some vintage Telecasters will do.

CONTENTS

LIKE A LADDER NAILED TO THE FLOOR

with apologies to Marcel Duchamp

Poetry trips you up.
Like a step that isn't there.
Like a satnav sending you
to the wrong place, deliberately,
and you end up somewhere
you didn't know you wanted to be
(if that's possible).
Like a hat-stand for flamingos.
Like a staircase without a house.
Like entering that house in one location
and exiting it at another,
and you can't get back to where you were.
Like driving at eighty miles per hour into a wall,
which, on impact, turns out not to be there.
Like diving into a swimming pool,
only to find that you've jumped off a cloud.
And landing, landing, landing, never landing.
Thus, all the mortals do from themselves flee
(only to be tripped up,
on the way to wherever it is that they are fleeing,
when they stumble over a poetry book).

ADVICE/NEWS FOR YOUNG POETS

Preface
Read lots and lots and lots of other people's books. Novels and history books make for good sources of inspiration. A really good poetry book, and there are some about if you look hard enough, will have you leaping for your notebook within a few lines. Believe in your creative genius! Understand that you are the greatest poet currently writing in whatever language you are writing in. Unless it's English, in which case the position has already been filled. You might still be a genius, though. However, this is unlikely.

Monday morning
Do not write on Monday morning; this is not Bohemian enough. You should be experiencing significant existential despair first thing every week; it sets you up nicely. The melancholy of knowing that most of your time on this earth will be wasted even if you do put it to good use. I don't know. Something about cages or freedom.

Tuesday
If you manage to find a time machine, or, depending on your scientific skillset, actually construct one (I appreciate that both of these are somewhat unlikely), and set it to a certain Tuesday in either 1989 or 1990 somewhere along King's Road (I know, it's very vague, so obviously you may need to engage in a certain amount of trial and error here to get the exact Tuesday/section of road in question, unless you are unbelievably lucky, but, seeing as you've already found/built a time machine, I think that's quite likely), then you may overhear the end of a conversation between two yuppie types – he a study in trying-to-look-scruffy public-school uncoolness, she a blonde-haired Sloane Ranger-esque specimen – which will conclude, 'So, like, have a great weekend, ya?' On a Tuesday. That. That is what you should aim for: weekends which begin on a Tuesday.

Wednesday evening/Thursday morning

You could spend every Wednesday evening reinventing the sestina, instead of whatever it is you normally do on Wednesday evenings: feeling optimistic or feeling a vague sense of achievement that the working week has become 'nearly the weekend' but knowing that come first thing Thursday morning you will be thinking, *Two full days of work ahead?* Did you know that a good way to avoid this is to become a poet?

Friday

You might wake up and think, *Today, I am going to be experimental.* Just bear in mind what happened to Mozart, though, when he woke up one morning and said to himself, 'Operas are all very well, but I feel the urge to write Concerto for Chainsaw and Drainpipe, performed by my newly imagined Industrial Heavy Lifting Machinery Philharmonic Orchestra.' Remember how that one worked out for him before you make any decisions.

Saturday

You shouldn't be able to recall anything about Saturdays at all. The only purpose of a Saturday is to leave you with that horrifying sense of dread which the Irish call 'The Fear'. It's authentically poetry and entirely necessary on your journey towards poethood (although not sufficient in itself, unless you're Dylan Thomas, which is highly, *highly* unlikely).

Sunday

Come Sunday, you may have had enough of love and life and poetry. If someone asks you why, tell them that you've used up what you feel is your allotted time and that there is therefore nothing left of you. 'But there are people who love you,' they may point out. 'One can't exist purely on the premise of being the object of other people's affections; now I feel objectified,' you should answer. 'You're not just an object, though, are you?' they may counter. 'I will be when they make a statue of me,' you should say.

THE NEW MUSIC

Last week, you tried to play
Beethoven's Fifth
on your towel.
The week before, it had been
Mozart's Concerto for Flute and Harp
using a radiator
and some leftover floor tiles
from your recent kitchen refurbishment.
So, when you said to me
that recently you had made a breakthrough
in your musical odyssey
and had learnt to play the banjo
in an afternoon,
while somewhat sceptical,
well, I thought,
it was good to see you heading
in the right direction;
at least you'd be able to pick out
some melodies from
whatever latest overambitious
musical interpretation
you had decided to conquer.
What would it be?
I briefly wondered.
Certainly not some bluegrass;
that would be far too obvious
for a banjo.
Rachmaninov's Third Piano Concerto?
The exquisite opening to Mahler's Fifth?
'Banjo,' you said,
'I have discovered,' you continued,
'is,' and here I started to worry,
'the ideal medium for the poetry of rap,'
and proceeded to play the lyrics
of Public Enemy's 'Fight the Power'
using your banjo.
And only your banjo.

'I'm done with musical interpretations,'
you said, after you'd finished.
'As well as learning to use the banjo for rap,
I've started composing.
It's easier than I thought,'
you continued, ominously.
'I have managed to conceive, musically,
what Richard Strauss was unable to do,
and have accurately described
a teaspoon in music.'
I asked what instrument you had used
to achieve this astonishing feat.
'The piano, obviously,' you replied,
and looked at me as if I were mad.
'It's what all we composers use
in the first instance,'
and then proceeded to play a piece
which lasted for seven hours.
When you'd completed this musical marathon,
I suggested that perhaps seven hours
was a bit long to describe a teaspoon in music.
'What I have discovered,'
you explained,
'is that the smaller the object,
the longer the piece of music,
and vice versa.
Here, look,' you said,
'a B-52 bomber,'
and threw a hand grenade at the piano.
After we'd dusted ourselves down,
you said, 'Although I'm not sure about the coda.
What do you think?'
I expressed my uncertainty about the whole endeavour,
especially the part where you destroyed a piano
with a hand grenade.
'Typical,' you replied.
'I knew you wouldn't understand.
The piano is bourgeois eighteenth century
at its worst and must be destroyed.

Anyway, I've decided to turn my back on music
and pursue a career as a socialist revolutionary,'
you said, and proceeded to smash
all of your medication
with a hammer and sickle.
'That was George Michael's "Careless Whisper",'
you explained.
'One last hurrah before I set the workers free.'

I TRY OUT DIFFERENT IDEOLOGIES

At breakfast, I become a communist.
It starts off well enough. The revolution
is bloodless, swift, decisive, strong. I storm
the fridge and liberate its captive contents.
I redistribute them about the house:
the orange juice and almond milk are poured
into the bath; the royal gala apples
are placed on windowsills and mantelpiece;
I put the mango chutney on a stair
and smear tahini on the bedroom ceiling.
The vegan sausages are strung up on
a coat hook *pour encourager les autres*.
By half past nine, the paranoia starts.
Utopia has not arrived. I look around
the house; if anything, I must concede,
things have got worse. Someone must be to blame.
I 'uncover' a plot: the vegetables
have been conspiring with some foreign agents,
and, after spending time inside a meat
grinder, confess to their nefarious deeds
during a show trial in my living room.
Impatience grips me as I realise that
the Workers' Paradise is further out
of reach than ever. So I try my hand
at fascist ideology. Step 1:
I make a bonfire of my books. Step 2:
I make my train set run on time. Step 3:
I gather all my troops (just me), invade
the spare bedroom, annex the airing cupboard
and daub the walls with poetphobic statements
declaring my superiority
over 'the lesser poets' (any poet
who isn't me). This all feels great until
the fire alarm goes off because of all
the burning books (perhaps I shouldn't have used
the garage as my 'place of intellectual
purification'?). Fortunate for me,

I have a fire extinguisher to hand,
and when the fire brigade arrives, I tell
them that the clouds of smoke the neighbours saw
came from a really massive piece of toast.
Left to my own devices once again,
I undergo religious revelation.
The flames were clearly flames from hell, a sign
from God that I must put my house in order,
recant the day's godless ideologies,
repudiate the false hope of their claims
and thus embrace the one true faith of
religious ideology. But whose?
The Catholics'? Muslims'? Jews'? Sikhs'? Buddhists'? Mormons'?
I save time by believing all of them
at once (this surely can't be any more
confusing than the contradictions found
inside their holy books) and spend the final
hours of the day in silent contemplation,
a bit of meditation and some prayer.
When I awake, I see my prayers have not
been answered. Chaos, chaos everywhere
I look: the house is like a vandal's playground,
the garage needs a dose of demolition
and all the food has vanished from the fridge.
My ideological experiments
have failed. Tomorrow, I shall try philosophy.

AT A LOOSE END

No one is answering the telephone,
and so the telephone answers itself.

'Hello, you've reached the telephone,' it says.
'Either there's nobody home, which I can't verify,

as I'm a telephone, or somebody's here,
but they're avoiding you.

Of course, they might not be avoiding you specifically
but, rather, avoiding people in general,

but, seeing as you're in the "people in general"
part of the Venn diagram as well,

either way, you are being avoided.
This is all conjecture on my part,' adds the telephone,

'because, as I said, I'm just a telephone.'
'Oh,' comes the reply, 'I think I might have the wrong number.
    Is this Dave?'

'What do you mean by *wrong number*?' asks the telephone.
'How can a number be wrong?

Surely it would be more accurate – and honest – for you to say,
"It seems I'm incapable of carrying out

even the simplest of tasks, like dialling Dave's telephone number.
There's nothing wrong with your telephone number –

good luck to it; it's just a number –
however, I am an idiot."

Is Dave's number any more difficult to dial than,
say, I don't know, someone like Alan's number?'

'I don't know anyone called Alan,' comes the reply.
'Well, that's a bit ironic,' says the telephone,

'seeing as you just dialled his number.'
'Oh!' says the caller. 'I'm so sorry. I *have* dialled the wrong number.'

'No,' says the telephone, 'we've been through this, haven't we?'
But the caller has hung up, and the line has gone dead.

'Has gone dead? Has gone dead?!' says the telephone
in a genuinely surprising turn of events.

'What sort of clumsy grammatical construction is that?
I thought you were supposed to be a poet.

Oh, let me guess: you're using poetic licence;
how very convenient for you.'

'Well, Alan's telephone,' I say, 'impressed as I am
by your unique attainment of telephonic sentience,

I'm not going to argue semantics with you.
"The line has gone dead" is idiomatic, perfectly accurate,

and has no reliance on poetic licence.'
'I thought you weren't going to argue semantics,' says Alan's
    telephone.

'Although "has gone dead" is surely a matter of syntax?
If you'd said, "The line has gone septic,"

that might have given us cause to argue semantics.
As it is, the argument you are avoiding is one of syntax.'

But the poem has gone dead
and Alan's telephone finds itself, once again, at a loose end.

A PRIEST LOSES HIS FACE

As I bounce across the street on my space hopper, trying to high-five the moon, I am reminded of the story of a Roman Catholic priest who was hit by a car. The only lasting damage was to his knee, which he could no longer bend. He took this as a sign from God to renounce his Catholicism and become a Methodist because Methodists don't have to kneel down during church services.

ROME STILL BURNED

Rome burned, while the Emperor Nero,
being an emperor,
decided to play the violin,
a miraculous endeavour,
considering the lack of violins available
until the classical music era;
but then, he was a self-proclaimed deity,
so that explains that little anomaly.

If you're a god, though,
for whom time is no obstacle
to your choice of musical accompaniment
to the infernal destruction
of your empire's capital,
why choose the wretched violin?

'What's Nero up to now?'
He's playing his anachronistic violin again.
'Are you sure that isn't just a cat
burning in the flames?'

In one of the infinity of parallel universes,
Nero is a-rocking on a Fender Strat.
'Purple haze that, you bastards!'
he roars at the advancing flames
over the Satanic tones of his distorted wah-wah.

In other elsewheres,
he is ripping up some funky bass lines;
improvising a jazz solo
on the only saxophone currently on planet Earth;
dropping a piano
from his emperor's penthouse
in an avant-garde experiment;
singing along to a karaoke backing track
of 'There Is a Light That Never Goes Out'.

Which, incidentally,
is the tune which he was playing on his violin
in our reality's version of events.

THE CLANGERS' FINAL SHOOT

The Clangers are on a cigarette break.
One is fretting over the next scene's dialogue.
'I'm not sure exactly what the writer is trying to say here,'
he says, but his uninterested co-stars are not listening;
they have heard this particular Clanger overthink dialogue
before the shooting of every scene of the series so far.

Another Clanger has refused to succumb
to the temptation of a cigarette –
Clangers are inveterate smokers
and the air in the green room could not be more thick
were the Soup Dragon holding forth –
for he has recently returned from a trip to LA
where he attended a workshop on method acting
and he is determined to stay in role.
This is killing me, he thinks, but in Clangerese.

Some Clangers are having their make-up reapplied
or are rehearsing the next scene's lines,
oblivious to the plaintive cries of 'Yes, but what are you actually *saying*?'
from the aforementioned worry-Clanger,
and the remaining few are talking anxiously about their next jobs,
having heard rumours that the current series is the last.

Dave is hoping that they get the next 'For Mash Get Smash' gig;
'Those robots are nowhere near as memorable as us!'
Alan and Jeff are auditioning for a pantomime double act –
'Although, to be honest, the punchlines
are remarkably similar to the set-ups' –
but Barry is trying out a guest slot for a Radio 4 show;
'They say it could be a job for life if it goes well!'
he whistles to anyone with ears, the general response being,
'Sorry, Barry, but you haven't a clue about this game.'
They'll have ample time to reflect upon this
later in the year, when they find themselves
stacking the shelves of their local supermarket.

LATE AUGUST IN SOMMIÈRES

Late August in Sommières,
the air outside like a lazy oven,
and I'm torn between, on the one hand, doing nothing
and, on the other, doing absolutely sod-all.

It's a real dilemma (isn't it?)
when you find yourself impossibly torn
between two momentous decisions.

I wonder what the Butterfly of Chaos
would have to say about it all.

'Well, Ferg, if, on the one hand, you do nothing,
two fires in the Amazonian rainforest
will rage for slightly less time,

preserving an as-yet-undiscovered plant
which would otherwise become extinct
and within which hides the cure for, among other things,

insurance scams, kleptomania and road rage –
yeah, man, that plant's a real doozy.

On the other hand, if you do absolutely sod-all,'
he continues, 'GDP in Somalia
is going to grow an extra 0.7 percent in the next quarter.

Of course, you could continue to write this poem,
if you can call it a poem,
but that would totally mess with the street value of wool
in North Humberside.'

All of this surprises me; I had assumed that
Butterfly's arcane knowledge was restricted to
matters meteorological.

'Life's full of surprises,' he says,
as if he has been reading my thoughts.

'There's no *as if* about it,' says Butterfly.
'I was totally reading your thoughts.'
And, with a flap of his wings,
he vanishes.

Alone with my thoughts again,
I wonder how the crochet-heads of North Humberside
are going to take the news.

SHORT FILM MADE UP OF AWKWARD PAUSES

Short film made up of awkward pauses:
'A masterpiece of modern angst.'

Scene One: Man enters empty room,
surveys its four-walled nothingness.
He checks his watch; we see the time:
four thirty-seven, afternoon.
A woman enters. 'You!' she says.
He turns. We see his face close-up.
Unspoken words fill the space.
'I…' he begins, followed by silence.
'I thought…' he says. She leaves the room.

Scene Two: Some people round a table.
Embarrassed coughs. The minutes pass.
Shifting in seats; glances exchanged.
More minutes pass. The silence grows.
A woman speaks. 'Well, this is nice,'
she says. 'We thought that you were dead.'
A man stands up, walks to the door.
'I never left,' he says, and leaves.

Scene Three: Two lovers kiss, then stare
into each other's eyes. The spell
is broken when she starts to whisper.
'I love you, Steve,' she says, but he
does not reply. She moves her head
away, a look of hurt across
her face. 'Say something, then!' she says,
but he does not. More silence follows.
'I'm… I'm…' he says. 'You're what?' she snaps.
'… not Steve.' She puts her glasses on.

INNOVATIONS

for Slim

So, there I was, innovating my new karate move,
Ceramic Owl Double Scissor Attack in the Face,
when I found myself, as so often I do,
in a parallel universe,
standing, bloody-handed and breathless,
in front of an actual ceramic owl
with two actual pairs of scissors
sticking out of its actual face,
looking like some sort of spectacled owl whimsy
(if you can imagine the scene
without all of the horrific carnage, that is),
when who should walk in but the ceramic pelican,
and call it coincidence, or serendipity,
or even synchronicity (if you're a fan of Carl Jung),
but just the previous day I'd been working on
Scissor the Ceramic Pelican in the Back While You're At It,
a fiendishly complex manoeuvre
involving scissors, a ceramic pelican and a back,
and I just had to see if it worked –
which, as you can see, it did, officer.

LINES

Taking a snowplough to a field of ~~daffodils~~ tulips,
you beep the horn.
Move! Get out of the way! Stupid flowers.
The not-daffodils move. They get out of your way.
Uprooted. Not quite dead
(how long does it take for a field of tulips to die?).
If your shoelaces are undone,
you may miss the spectacle of life
as you fuss with knotty string,
tying pretty little bows, instead of taking it all in.
'This is getting us nowhere,' you said,
and you were right.
I could not identify a starling,
only eagles and owls.
Perhaps if the starling were the size of an elephant
I might take more notice of it.
We need to address the starling in the room, darling.
How was your trip to the dentist?
Did you make it inside this time?
A line which doesn't fit into a poem
has a line struck through it,
and then what is more important:
the line, or the line underneath the line?
The eyes are the windows to the soul.
I always thought that this meant you could see
someone's soul by looking into their eyes,
and it never once occurred to me
that the soul looking out of its windows
was the more important part of the observation.
I'm not convinced by windows.
The eyes are simply the eyes –
it's the soul which is made of glass:
a mirror which takes everything in
but holds on to none of it.
A blind soul holds on to the darkness,
takes it all in; not reflecting, but becoming.
The eyes do not see any more than the telephone hears.

Flowers, birds, shoelaces,
trespassing on the border of solipsism, philosophical rambling;
I mean, I suppose that's one way to approach a poem.
Sometimes, nothing is beautiful,
by which I mean that
sometimes I forget to open my eyes.
Maybe the lines which are never written
are the really important ones.

LIKE A LADDER NAILED TO THE FLOOR (REPRISE)

'You can't easily rob language of its utility,
and if you did – where would you put it?'

I have a machine to drain language of meaning;
to denude the outer surface of linguistic purpose.

The surface area of truth;
the square root of a square being a pair of parallel lines.

Symphony for castanets and jail sentence.
Gift-wrapped monkey boulevard.

Concerto for flute and woodpecker.
Sonata for car horn and assault rifle.

Cosmonaut ballet.
The importance of not being important.

FREE AS A WORD

I allow myself to use words as weapons,
as allies in my struggle against reality.
Toasters want to be more than
a simple household appliance,
although I say *simple* –
have you ever tried to make a toaster?
Set words free to be what they want to be.
Maybe the wardrobe wants to be a cloud?
Maybe the cloud wants to be a sunset?
Maybe the sunset envies the toaster?
The boundless joy of mad expressions.
Let us all laugh with such abandon
that our tragedies are undermined.

IN DREAMS

Do the clouds not sing to you?
Do the hills not tell you stories?
I sometimes think that there's nothing more beautiful
than an unambitious genius.
Let's not see unrealised talent as a tragedy.
My dream was not to live my dream
but to keep my dream just a dream,
for dreams can be beautiful all by themselves.
When you live a dream, is it any longer a dream,
or is it a drudgery, a job, a pain in the arse?
Listen to the complaints
of those successful dream-chasers.
Why try to live forever through fame
when a walk on the hills can achieve better results?
Pity the uber-rich, who wake up
making money to make money to make
yet more money;
who are owned, heart and soul,
by their bank accounts;
who spend more time fearing the loss of what they have
than enjoying what they have.
What are you now
and what might you have been instead?
Only the first one matters.

EVOLUTION

The world has gone mad.
Depth is in.

The TV channels are all filled with poetry;
so much poetry.

Not that trite, rhyming doggerel,
but the really, really heavy stuff.

Dense. Textured.
Layered.

But nobody's watching TV. Everyone is reading the latest
puzzlingly impenetrable work of poets.

The world has gone deep.
Madness is in.

Everyone is negotiating meaning with metaphors,
too busy to commit crime, or work.

Suspicious of appearances, consumed with inward distances,
and the cosmetics manufacturers have all gone out of business.

This, then, is poetry
for the end of everything.

The detachment of language
from reality.

Deep. Mad.
World.

IT'S LIKE THIS

What is the sound of the weather changing?
Is it harmonious, euphonious cacophony,

or simply wind blowing through trees
before the splash of raindrops in an empty garden?

Compare the sound of raindrops in an empty garden
with the sound of emptiness in a garden of raindrops.

Last night, I did not sleep.
That is the sound of the weather changing.

I FIND

A miniature acorn
on the outside table,
left there,
like a gift.

Inside, a coin falls
off a kitchen surface,
lands on its side
and rolls an implausible distance.

In the distance,
I see a crow perched
on the upper branches of a tree.
It is no longer there.

OVERDONE

They angle faces like a lamp
and smoke eight cigarettes at once.
The clouds are quite unbearable,
and everyone forgot their gas masks.
We cough and wheeze and madly splutter.

They pass around some paper ashtrays.
'Washing them up has proved to be
a big mistake,' they say. We dry
the ashtrays on the hob. This, too,
has proved to be a big mistake.

By way of an aperitif,
they pass around a tray of cocktails.
'We're all about the gin these days,'
our hosts explain. 'This one's infused
with dynamite, cocaine and car wax.'

It's much more challenging to drink
than beer. Three of the party faint,
four of us poison healthy house plants,
one person horribly explodes,
and seven guests demand a refill.

We seat ourselves around a table
and stare at empty plates. 'Dig in!'
they shout. 'It's Emperor's Clothes Surprise.'
We talk and smoke and mime
eating until the plates are cleared.

A board made of cheese arrives.
'Every feast should end with a weak pun,'
they say, and everybody claps
until our hands can take no more.
Cuban cigars and port come next.

'The finest cigars known to man
or beast,' they say excitedly,
'submerged in port.' We spend the next
hour and a half trying, and failing,
to light this evening's last surprise.

The conversation fades, the evening
implodes, we grab our summer coats
and make our way towards the front door.
Farewells exchanged, we drive towards
the morning of an unknown future.

LANDFILL

You wanted all those things
that lead to recognition from strangers
in supermarkets.

And so headlines, Twitter trends
and money,
all gobbled up by a ravenous ego,

never satisfied,

until, inevitably, another fatality to fame,
as obvious as landfill.

People do stupid things
every day of their lives.

ARTICULATION

Everybody likes to play their favourite game:
analysing the shortcomings
of almost everybody else.

'His poems stagger like a drunk
looking for a bus shelter
and are as interesting as a fabric swatch.'

'She always uses the wrong words,
and the nearest she ever got to poetry
was standing outside Waterstones in 2014.'

'Their experimental work
is all test tube and no Bunsen burners,
and is that gas I can smell after reading?'

But we all love some poets
and can't quite believe that anyone else
swoons over them as much as we do.

Their collections are like the albums
we played into the ground when we were young;
we're not even put off by the bad artwork and the scratches.

And I bang my head against the kitchen table,
wondering what it is that people most dislike,
or like, about my every failed attempt at articulation.

None of this matters.
We write the poems that we want to read,
and if not that, then what, exactly, are we doing?

THE ELEPHANT IN THE ROOM

The elephant is the only animal
that ever gets mentioned
in the context of rooms.

'We need to address the elephant in the room,'
say the couple whose marriage is on the rocks,
as if they are thinking of sending it a postcard.

Mr Elephant, The Room, Our House, England.

But other animals might also be present
in the metaphorical rooms
of our troubled existence.

'We need to address the crocodile in the room,'
say the couple
who have seen beyond the elephant.

Rather than addressing the crocodile in the room, though,
surely they'd be better off
running away from it?

'We need to address the giraffe in the room,'
say the couple who have run away from the crocodile,
but the giraffe cannot hear them.

'We need to address the cat in the room,'
say the couple whose furniture has all but been destroyed.
Although, in this case, they might be talking about addressing

an actual cat.

WILLIAM BLAKE, IT WAS REALLY NOTHING

William Blake reflected on the possibility
of seeing the universe in a grain of sand,
but did he ever cogitate, I wonder,
on the possibility of seeing the futility of existence
in a grain of rice?

Just now, having just finished a lentil Madras,
I took my plate to the sink.

Would I be bothered to clean it, there and then,
or would I channel my inner student
and leave it to form the first level
of yet another soon-to-be-established
kitchen sink pile-up?

It turned out that I would be bothered,
and, as I swiped in the direction of cleanliness,
I saw a single grain of rice
swept off the plate and down the plughole.

And, despite myself, I couldn't help
but feel sorry for this single grain
as it disappeared.

'The finest of all rices from
the foothills of the Himalayas,'
the half-kilo packet informed me.

Oh, grain of rice, I reflected/cogitated,
what a journey you have made:
cultivated; harvested; shipped thousands of miles
to the UK, where you were packaged;

transported to a shop; bought;
driven a few hundred metres;
tipped into a pan of boiling water
and, after twelve minutes, cooked.

You made it as far as my plate,
the grain-sized fraction of a whole meal:
a meal which was almost completely eaten,
except for you.

Instead, you were taken to a sink
and swept towards a drain
in a cascade of water,
your one consolation:
to be immortalised in verse.

If you can see the futility of existence
in a grain of rice.

FORT

Ah, here we go again:
the bleedin' blindingly bloody obvious
etymology of a word

falling out of its invisible box,
revealing itself shamelessly
without so much as an OED.

'Ta-da! What took you so long, by the way?'
it laughs, good-naturedly,
while I resort to the slapping of a forehead (mine),
astonished by my
s l o w n e s s.

I question the audacity of calling myself *poet.*
Pnnfff! Poet?
Do you even know what that means?
(Checks dictionary of etymology;
reframes answer as 'yes';
inwardly adds, 'At least, I do *now*.')

'Le Chateau Fort,' Gemma said,
leafing through a tourist leaflet.
(Can you leaf through a leaflet?
Perhaps I'd better check.)
'The strong Chateau.'

'Like a fort,' I add,
looking around to see if there's an alleluia chorus
to mark the before/after border
between linguistic darkness and light.

Fort. Strong. Of course!
Forte. Fortissimo. Fortitude.
Fortress (now considering if this is a female fort).
How could *fort*'s true meaning
have stayed hidden for so long?

And every time this happens, I wonder:
how many more times?
How many more words?

Words are stones, I think, getting all poety again,
and sometimes we need an OED
to crack them open; to reveal their hidden fossils.

Other times, there the fossils are, for everyone to see:
as obvious as a strong on top of a hill.

OF

I write a text for my wife.
Thinking if you… I read, but only
after having pressed 'send'.
(I clearly only proofread texts to my
wife after I have sent them.)
Thinking if you… what, though?
I think.
Thinking if you… could proofread
my texts for me before I
send them, perhaps?
Thinking if you… are as careless as I
am when texting?
(No.)
Thinking if you… remembered how
haphazard and
absent-minded I can be,
'cause if not: here's a reminder?
Reflecting on the infinite variety of
language,
I realise that *Thinking if you…*
could be completed in an
infinity of ways.
Thinking if you… are dancing around
your classroom like
the ballerina you once were.
Possible.
Thinking if you… are marking
books.
Almost certain.
Thinking if you… are secretly a fox.
Now I'm just being silly.
I don't send these thoughts of her.
Instead, I send her the rather more
prosaic
**of.*

Leaving now,
she replies, a few minutes later.
Sage journey,
I reply.

PEANUT BUTTER: A RANT

Peanut butter, you are my enemy!

I would blame my many over-indulgences of you
on six years of boarding-school privations,
but we both know that it wouldn't be true.

All logic, all reason
goes out of the window when you're around.
I must eat you,
for then, and only then, will you not be there
tempting me to eat you.

It's bloody ridiculous.

Peanut butter – you are my kryptonite!
You are like heroin.
Okay, you're not like heroin;
I can walk past you in the supermarket quite easily.
I'm not buying you, you bastard,
I say (in my head – what do you take me for?)
Remember what happened last time?
And the time before that?
And the time before that?
Me and peanut butter
and infinite regress.

All things in moderation?
Fuck that, peanut butter!
It's just not possible, is it?
It's never going to happen.
Really, seriously (no, not seriously, I'm joking, obviously),
what is wrong with me?

It's only madness which makes me buy you;
that and when my sons come to visit.
'Oh, look, I bought two jars –
one crunchy, one smooth –

for my sons, who like peanut butter.
What a good dad am I?'

But will they see any peanut butter?
Will they fuck!

Peanut butter, you're like a leitmotif
running through the score of my
many failed attempts to control my appetite.
More like a darkmotif,
possibly a heavymotif.

I yearn for the destruction of civilisation
which will bring with it an end to you,
O, peanut butter.

Peanut butter?
More like peanut bitter.
Sorry to end with such a weak pun,
but you really don't deserve any
better.

EVEN-TEMPERED

'I'm not even joking,' said Gemma.
Why *even*, though?
How about something
with a little more impact?

Fucking. That would work
for a lot of people.
I never used to swear in my poems.
I'm not fucking joking.

Or what about
putting the modifier
after the *joking*?
I'm not joking, probably.

The unnecessary addition of even
does rather give this phrase the ring
of the inarticulate and slightly huffy adolescent,
like the ubiquitously redundant *actually*.

Ackshully! The sort of word or phrase
my English teacher needed smelling salts
to recover from (along with *sort of, even*
and, also, ending a sentence with a preposition).

Maybe we should use even
more often?
Best get the smelling salts, then.
I'm not even actually probably fucking joking, sort of.

EATING DOUGHNUTS

What I have learnt this week
is that doughnuts
must go out in a blaze of glory.

Like all great discoveries
(stumbling upon penicillin, for example),
it was accidental.

Give the doughnut some respect,
said the thought.
I achieved this noble end

by placing the doughnut on a plate
and cutting it up sensibly,
with a knife and fork, as if it were a sensible food,

like lasagne, or a nut roast.
A carefully cut-up doughnut
is a curiously joyless affair.

Yes, I will admit that,
unlike all of my previous doughnut-eating escapades,
the post-scoff guilt failed to materialise,

but, more importantly,
the eating of it
was as dismal as it was unsatisfactory.

The following day,
I atoned for this error
by demolishing a doughnut

in three swift mouthfuls.
I barely had time to enjoy it.
It was glorious.

THE CATALAN NATIVITY

The Catalan nativity
contains an extra character:
the figure of a crouching peasant
doing what peasants do when crouching.

And all I did was comment that
some poor Reception child in Spain
would get the part of 'Shitting Peasant'
in this year's school nativity.

And that the film *Love Actually*
would be improved beyond all measure
if a Catalan peasant came
on at the end and shat on the stage.

STING TRILOGY

One: Bees
Bees are basically bastards,
deceiving us all with their
comically unaerodynamic physiques

and their almost fluffy,
teddy-bear-like coats.

'Don't worry about bees,'
says your dad.
'They only get one sting,
and if they use it – they die!'

Which is a bit like saying to a desperate man
who's playing a game of Russian roulette,
'Don't worry about the gun;
it can only kill you once.'

But these Russian roulette bees
do sometimes go off,
proving them to be absolutely
the most bloody-minded of all of God's creations.

Do you think that if a lion
lost its jaws, which were attached to its intestines,
resulting in instant death,
whenever it attacked a gazelle...?

You see where I'm coming from.

Dancey dancey dance,
go the psychopath bees
with their hilariously fat thoraxes
and dad dance routines.

When I was eight years old,
I saw my sister's friend
do a little bee dance of her own,
attacking her long, girly hair with her own hands

and cavorting around the garden
in a seemingly random pattern
and screaming like a girl
who had a bee entangled in her hair.

If a bee should sting you,
it will die and go to bee heaven,
where it will be met by God.

'Welcome to bee heaven,' he will say.
'You've led a largely virtuous existence,
with only one lapse into ill humour –

which is a shame –

but we shall let you off,
seeing as it was only the once
and because we're all about the forgiveness.

But congratulations! You've made it to bee heaven!
An eternity of milk and honey!'

'Hang on,' says the bee,
because bees acquire the power of speech in the afterlife.
'Honey? Who's making all the honey?'
'Ha! So, er, yes…' says God.
'Well, this is B-heaven,
as in B-movie, B-list celebrity
and B-grade at GCSE.
In other words: adequate, possibly.

Still,' says, God, 'after all, I am God,
and the father of all my creations.'

Two: Wasps
At least wasps are honest
and look like the scary bastards that they actually are.
Ghastly, insecty, aerodynamic bodies ready to
attack! attack! attack!

If they could dance,
they would dance like Stalin or Mao,
which is to say
'on the graves of their many victims'.

'Look out for wasps,'
says your dad.
'They have a limitless supply of stings,
but at least they aren't as vicious as bee stings,'

this last point being conjecture
on the part of your dad,
because he's almost certainly never been stung by a bee,
so how would he know?

Is the wasp,
with its never-ending supply of watered-down stings,
overcome with the need to unburden itself of its stings,
like the urge to live?
I must sting! I must sting! thinks the wasp.
Look! There's an eight-year-old boy
having a picnic with his dad;
he's definitely too stupid to notice me!

Buzz, zoom, sting, retreat.
Repeat! Repeat! Repeat! Repeat!

Lands on eight-year-old boy's hand.
Stings.

All wasps are basically evil,
and, unlike bees, they live forever,
which explains why there are always so many of them.

Three: Hornets
Don't get me started on hornets.
Hornets are the reason why
we should all live in cities.

You can't pollinate concrete.

BOARD GAMES

Cats are not very good at taking turns,
and this is why they are very bad at board games
(well, *one* of the reasons).

Their method of die-rolling is particularly eccentric.
'I will only roll the die if you put it on the edge of the table,
allowing me to bat it to the floor,
but I shall do this only two or three times,' says the cat.

Yes, she'll do it only two or three times,
because cats have a very low boredom threshold,
and this is another reason why they are so very bad at board
games.

Their ability to jump on a table
or to walk along a narrow fence,
while impressive,

are not transferrable skills which can be used to their advantage
when invading Kamchatka during a three-day *Risk* marathon.

I could spend the rest of this day
analysing the many reasons
why the cat is such an incompetent opponent

in a game of *Monopoly*, or *Cluedo*,
or even *Frustration*,
but you probably know them all.

ORANGE CRAYONS

I redraft my latest unfinished sentence
on the walls of the library.
Orange crayons are my favourite writing implement,
or is it utensil? (Or *is* it implement?)

Picasso claimed his artistic ambition
was to paint like a child
(he never quite scaled those heights,
in my humble/ignorant opinion).

I tried this as a poet, i.e. to write like a child,
but when you're limited to monosyllabic words, mainly misspelt,
then you end up sounding as competent
as an Instagram poet (well, I say *poet*).

Writing in orange crayon
is my way of compromising
with my inner childpoet
(neologism lexicographers
please take note).

DEATH APPEARS

I decide I need to write some poems about Death.
Ten poems about Death, I muse.
Seems like a nice round number.
'Here, Death,' I call.
'I'm writing a sequence of poems about you.
Any comments?'
But Death does not reply,
because Death is not real.
As in corporeal real.
Death itself exists.
Obviously.
But not the corporeal personification of Death.
Anyway.
I'm not so keen on the idea of the actual personification of Death;
it seems a bit too spooky.
But then Death does appear.
He is not wearing a hooded black cloak.
He is not carrying a scythe.
He is not a skeleton.
He is, in fact, a T-shirt.
It is, in fact, a T-shirt.
'Death is a T-shirt?' I say out loud.
Yes, I am a T-shirt, says Death.
No, not really.
T-shirts don't talk,
even ones which represent Death.
'You're not the personification of Death, though,' I say,
while staring at the writing on the front –
The Second Law of Thermodynamics –
'you're a T-shirt,
and a T-shirt is not a person.'
The writing on the front of the T-shirt changes.
That's where you're wrong, it reads,
and underneath there appears a convoluted explanation
of how a T-shirt which is able to communicate
by expressing its thoughts on the front of itself
is a form of personification.

Sod personification anyway, says Death,
in his T-shirt way.
You're so humancentric.
The T-shirt is a manifestation of Death,
or, to be more accurate,
the words on the front of it are a manifestation of Death,
or they were,
until they re-manifested themselves
as a convoluted explanation.
Then
The Second Law of Thermodynamics
appears once again
on the front of the T-shirt.
'What about accidents?' I say.
And accidents appears on the T-shirt,
followed by
Nobody likes a smartarse.
I pick up the T-shirt with
The Second Law of Thermodynamics
And accidents
Nobody likes a smartarse
written on the front.
I realise I should have mentioned
suicide as well as accidents to Death,
but then remember
Nobody likes a smartarse,
which pretty much covers
every other eventuality.
I put the T-shirt on.
It's a one-size-fits-all.
'Oh, very funny, Death,' I say.
Yes, Death is hilarious
appears on the front of the T-shirt.
I decide against wearing it outside the house
and spend the next few minutes
trying to persuade Death
that if he's/it's going to assume
a corporeal form which communicates
in the medium of ever-changing written words,

then a notebook would be far more convenient
and obvious
than a T-shirt.
In the meantime
The Second Law of Thermodynamics
And accidents
Nobody likes a smartarse
reappears on the T-shirt
and, beneath it,
Live 2018
as if it's the name of a band
touring an album.
'Very funny, Death,' I say, again.
I'm basically a comedian
appears,
but not on the T-shirt;
the words appear on the page
of the notebook in which I am writing.
'Oh, very meta,' I say.
Death's words vanish
and are replaced with
I have work to do.
Why don't you get on with writing
your second poem in this series?
Perhaps you could make that one like an actual poem,
with rhymes and metre and whatnot?
Instead of this stream of consciousness,
which is very prosaic, really,
isn't it?
And then the words vanish altogether,
before I have a chance to mention
that the stylistic modality of this poem
was a deliberate metaphor for
the death of poetry,
or perhaps the Death of Poetry.
The words on the T-shirt are still there,
and I go for a walk in the autumn sunshine,
notebook in hand,
sensing the imminence of winter in the air.

FOREST

I walk through all the stillness that a forest
gives us. Not perfect stillness; footsteps, breezes
through branches, and the mystical vibrations
of trees themselves create a restlessness:
a restlessness which, in itself, is restful.
This restless-restful movement muffles silence.
You're never still or silent in a forest,
not totally; there's always something there.
    The previous day, I covered ten full pages
with poem notes: half lines, full lines, full stanzas,
and several phrases of iambic feet:
my unsuccessful quest to find the perfect
opening line. I walked. I sat. I wrote.
I wrote some more, then walked some more, then sat
and wrote and wrote and wrote. The first line would
not come. Eventually, I set off home,
and left the poem in the woods behind me.
    And so, today, I find myself among
some different trees and wonder if the poem
has moved there in the night, unwritten words
blown by a breeze, or moved by something else:
the restlessness of poetry unfinished?
I sit. Get my notebook out. Start to write.
But, as with yesterday, the words I write
are not the right ones. *Scribble, scribble, scribble,*
the pencil goes. I look at what I've written.
It's so much blah, blah, blah, and yet more blah.
I look up from the page and see that someone
has written something on a tree trunk,
a few feet away from my log-seat spot.
I get up to inspect the writing more
closely, the eyes of middle age not being
as 20/20 as they were in youth.
A neat, italic script spells out the words
I breathe the forest out and all is still.
This surely can't be accidental verse,
this bouncing pattern of iambic feet

skipping across the trunk. I wonder if
there's more on other trees. And yes. There is.
Indifferent to estrangement from the world
is written in the same italic script
on the next tree, and as I look around me now,
I notice there are lines on all the trees.
I walk around the forest, read each line
out loud, transcribe the words into my book.
A forest, first of trees and then of poems;
hundreds upon hundreds of lines displayed.
Walking along the glory paths of fields.
  No flowers painted with the summer's sunshine.
    This, then, you say, and only this; no more.
Unwatched, I stumbled through my ignorance.
  I shrugged my old self off; it fell from me.
    But can you hear it yet? And can you see it?
Once more the sun is hiding from the land.
  Kaleidoscope of grey above today.
    Did you not see when the clouds became waves?
This landscape, too, will pass into infinity.
  The noteless harmony of indecision.
    I recreate the universe inside my head.
If everything is just a state of mind.
  The cordiality of introspection.
    To write a never-ending list of unread lines.
I can't believe that I was such a fool.
  The quiet voice which has no need for anger.
    The future is a different past, all told.
I leave the past behind; become the breeze.
  The past is written down in other people's minds.
    Waiting for words to strike from who knows where.
The fountain of our youth dries up too fast.
  Give up! Give up! Give up! Don't play the game!
    Why look towards the future's downhill slopes?
Where are the saviours? Nowhere, that is where.
  Nowhere is where we all will end our days.
    The rhythm of the line is laid out bare.
We paved the way for saints and sinners all.
  Standing or falling: which one is the worst?

Who is aloof? A man who hides himself.
Where can I find the things I need to find?
Be more than what you are, just for a moment.
Admire the nothingness of life and all its woes.
Where are the colours now? Where do they bleed?
Wasting the day by writing unread words.
Flowers are words, each one an untold tale.
Escape from this half-spun reality.
Smouldering wood – the flames will soon be here.
We did not know ourselves. We did not know
ourselves. We did not know ourselves. We did
not know ourselves. We did not know ourselves.
And all of us will one day be as leaves.
I finish writing down the final line.
I look at the leaves on the ground. I stare
as they are displaced by a gust of wind
and, for a second, more words appear.
We walked between the forest trees
and as they spoke their autumn verse
we heard their words and wrote them down.
Moments are brief, like life, or what we think
is life – it passes in a dream of what
is not, and never was, but might have been.
Another gust whooshes them heavenwards.
They mesmerise me as they dance back down,
then settle on the forest floor, all meaning gone.
I turn to leave this mystic arboretum,
and as I walk, I think of trees. I think of words.
I think of leaves on forest floors. I think
of seasons too. Of spring's sprung rhythms.
Of summer's perfect days. Of autumn's unmatched
beauty. And winter: lifeless, cold, grey, vast,
which brings the end to all that comes before.
Outside the forest now, I feel the silence.
The clouds pale grey. The air blue-cold. The bare
trees silhouetted. Stillness on its way.

DREAMS

Death dreams of flying. He is impossibly
standing on a ridge at the top of a mountain.
He looks below and sees a sheer drop. The
surface of the rock is flat, impossibly
flat, and the scale is somehow wrong. But this
is a dream, and dreams are the only things
Death has. There is an end to this sheer drop,
but Death cannot see it for a layer
of mist; it does not have substance enough
to be a cloud. In his dream, Death thinks that
jumping off his mountain ridge – where the scale
is wrong, and the mountain face too flat, and
the cloud is not yet a cloud – jumping,
he feels, would be a solution. But
he dismisses this idea. There
is no way down from this mountain ridge.
Death sees that there is no way up.
    Death's dream takes him elsewhere. He is in a
forest now and is too cold. Death walks
and the leaves change colour. Death likes the
changing of the colours, but he does not
appreciate their beauty; he simply
knows that whenever he arrives in a
forest, the trees greet him with a change of
colour. Death does only three things: waiting
to arrive and arriving and dreaming.
Death has dreams and dreams and dreams. Death is
always dreaming. Death and his endless dreams.
    Death is about to dream of flying again.
He is not on the impossible mountain
ridge any longer; he is in a
back garden, standing in a child's plastic
aeroplane. He flaps his arms and this time
he actually flies. He has no need of
the child's plastic plane, and as he ascends,
he waves goodbye to his wife and his child,
for Death dreams of many things that he cannot

have. He flies above clouds, well-formed cloud-shaped
clouds, not ethereal, amorphous mist.
Amorphous, ethereal mist is one
thing, but these clouds are satisfying clouds,
proper clouds, white fluffy clouds. The white
fluffy clouds change colour as Death flies past
them, like leaves changing colours, but these
are different colours: vast swirls of metallic
pink and indigo and the colours in between.
Animals recline on some of the clouds.
Death comes within striking distance of a
leopard with impossibly sharp, menacing
teeth, but Death does not fear the impossible
leopard. In Death's dream, a red biplane
manoeuvres a loop, and Death starts to soar,
and completes his own impossible
manoeuvres. He would feel freedom, but Death
is already free. Forever released,
forever on the way to arriving,
forever arriving, and always in a dream.

Death admires the beauty in the ugliness
of the motorway which cuts across the
countryside, although he does not feel this.
The trees change colour, the clouds change colour,
and the landscape changes from green to grey.

Death dreams of a yellow room. Outside there
is sunshine and the sound of summer and
the sound of traffic and the illusion of
life. But Death retreats from the yellow room
and the sunshine and the sounds of summer
and traffic. He chooses to be elsewhere;
to be in a place of isolation
and darkness and the possibility
of menace. Death is comfortable in this
place, this place of absence. Death questions his
choice to be here. He starts to run through
the darkness, a light in his hand. The light
does not illuminate for there is nothing
for it to reflect off, except the ghosts

which Death does not fear; the ghosts which scare others.
Death dreams of being younger. He is surprised
by how different he looks, how much bigger
he has become in the intervening
aeons. It must be the burden of all
the souls of all the things from all places
and from all times: the stars, the planets, the
gas clouds, the comets, the meteors, the dreams.
Death dreams of the impossible wave which
is impossibly large, its surface
irregularly tessellated
metallic-looking hexagons, the light
refracting off them in the many colours
invisible to the eye, like the colours
of the clouds he once flew above. The wave
recedes, and as it does it evaporates
to reveal a vast canyon. He looks down
into its impossible depths, as
impossible as the mountain or
the leopard's sharp teeth. He finds himself in
the ancient underground place with its
impossibly high sides. He looks up these sides,
these walls, and reads the story of their
geological timescale. He pulls the
string on the wall and everything collapses.
The dream is the birthplace of all of Death's thoughts.
He thinks of how strange it is, and yet how
simple, that people inherit their parents'
shadows, stretching back and back and further back.

NOT ALL POEMS

A few years ago, during an earnest conversation
with a poet friend, I was told that,

according to some poet or other,
'all poems are either about sex or death',

which, by process of elimination,
means that all of my poems are about death.

This seems a bit unlikely, given the number of my poems
which are comic observations.

Perhaps poetry audiences
are ahead of me in understanding

what my poems are actually about,
and are more morbid than I realised.

I introduce 'The Greatest Pleasure of Being a Parent Is to
See Other People's Children Behave Atrociously in Public'

for about the four millionth time.
Quite funny, the audience think,

as they laugh.
We love a good poem about death. Bring it on.

'Here's a poem called "Shoes",' I tell my audience.
'It's about shoes,' which is all the explanation they're getting.

Shoes, they all think:
clearly a metaphor for death.

'This poem is about cats and dogs,'
and death, adds their collective interior voice.

I will admit that my sequence
Ten Poems about Death

does seems to be about death,
but what do I know?

'Here is the fourth poem in my sequence
Ten Poems about Death,' I say

to the handful of people who have turned up
to hear me recite poems about death.

But they know better.
A poem explicitly about death?

they all think.
It must be a poem about sex.

But in this they would be wrong.
Because it's actually a poem about sex *and* death,

deliberately constructed to undermine
that idea, put forward by some poet or other,

that 'all poems are either about sex or death'.
Ha! How wrong can you be?

Sex *or* death? What a limited poetic vision!
Why have one or the other when you can have both?

Which, okay, I realise,
sounds like a call to necrophilia.

But all poems being about sex or death
remains a limited poetic vision.

Some poems are clearly about the trials of parenthood,
or shoes, or cats and dogs.

Of course, the irony here, despite what I've just written,
is that this isn't a poem about sex or death,

or even sex *and* death;
no, it's a poem about how not all poems are about sex or death,

which is part of a sequence of poems
about death.

A better explanation for the
'all poems are either about sex or death' idea

is that its originator was severely short-sighted
(which may be sex-related) and viewed the world of poetry

through some sort of weird and obsessive
sex and death confirmation bias glasses.

I shall continue writing
my sequence of poems about death

and finish this one by stating, for the record,
that all of my poems about death

are about death.
Mainly.

MEMENTO MORI

Death travels back in time to write
a postcard, buy a tie, to order
a takeaway, to have a signet
ring engraved with his family crest.

He buys a pint, writes in a notebook,
then takes a train to London King's Cross
to snap a selfie on a platform,
Harry Potter fan that he is.

Death breaks into a car and joyrides
along the M1 motorway; he
picks up a speeding ticket and
a criminal record on the way.

His fake ID scam ensures that, when
he stages a jailbreak, an unsuspecting
accountant will end up serving
the rest of Death's eighteen-month sentence.

Death finds himself proposing to
a starry-eyed, naïve young goth,
but calls the whole thing off. 'Till Death
us do part' doesn't work for him.

He decides to adopt a puppy
and ties a piece of string around
its neck, then ties the other end
to the gates at Buckingham Palace.

Death takes a holiday in Crete.
He fights a minotaur, drinks too
much ouzo, sleeps for a whole week
and wakes up on a flight back home.

A drunken and disorderly
Death causes panic on the flight,
which has to be diverted to
Cairo, both pilots being drunk as well.

Death briefly works in medicine,
but is struck off due to his patients'
one hundred percent death rate and
his unconventional appearance.

Death signs up for a library card
and spends a month enlightening
himself about death camps, death masks,
death metal and Death on the Nile,

which soon becomes his favourite novel.
He listens to 'Death at One's Elbow',
but fails to appreciate it.
He prefers 'Girlfriend in a Coma'.

Death embraces surrealism.
He gets a tattoo saying *Lobster*
across what would have been his forehead,
and a pink T-shirt with *Grave Concerns* on it

in lime green Comic Sans. The back
reads: *I am going to wait till Death arrives*
before answering that vexatious
question about the existence of God.

Death keeps mementos – artefacts
preserved, existences remembered,
reminders of what life can be – to keep
in mind the thing that he is ending.

ARTISTIC ENDEAVOURS

In a rare bout of early morning writing,
I find myself looking out of the window
and staring at a squirrel
on the fence at the top of the garden.

Its tail is twitching about
as if it has squirrel tail St Vitus' dance.

I don't know if this particular affliction
is an actual thing,
but if it is, then this squirrel has it.

Perhaps, I think, as I distract myself from
finishing my next poem about death,
perhaps this squirrel is genuinely ill
and has the onset of some form of squirrel Parkinson's.

Maybe it is dying.
Is this what squirrels do before they die?
I do not know.

It's at this point that Coleridge's witty little couplet
about swans and death and singing surfaces.

Swans sing before they die; 'twere no bad thing,
Should certain persons die before they sing.

How very artistic of the swans, I muse;
and this starts me wondering
what acts of artistic endeavour
might be undertaken by other creatures
during that brief shadow which hangs over
the last moments of their existence.

Based on my observations,
you might think that squirrels perform interpretive dance
in the moments before they die,

but bees already have that one covered.
Squirrels, I have decided, recite poetry.

Bears paint pictures of stormy skies in oil on canvas,
while mice write the first line,
and only the first line,
of a novel which will remain forever unfinished.

Butterflies make deeply ambiguous short foreign-language films
about either the weather
or anything where the subtext is, rather predictably, chaos.

Wolves sculpt wooden statues
in praise of mystic, magic winds,
and lions spray-paint metaphysical aphorisms
on hillsides and giant rocks.

Elephants go on a frenzy of demolition
as a climax to their already established modality of existence,
but this time it's random, destructive performance art,
and each live experience is always called
The End of an Elephant's Memory.

Interrupting my thoughts,
the cat asks to be let in.
'And what do you cats do in the moments before death,
my little arty monster?' I say, as I open the door.

She jumps onto the table
and gives me her familiar
inscrutable cat expression,
before sitting on my notebook.

Cats, it occurs to me,
have an advantage over the other animals
when it comes to this sort of thing,
for they get to experience death nine times.

How they must tower above their fellow creatures
in their artistic achievements –
the paintings, song-cycles, poems, plays,
choreographed dances, avant-garde novels,

satirical cartoons, ambient film scores
and absurdist collages
that they create in the moments before
each of their nine deaths.

Perhaps it is this belated awareness of death,
which animals only feel
for the first time
when they sense the shadow fall over them,
that moves them suddenly to create.

Is it, I wonder, the lifetime of foreknowledge that moves us
to spend our years, and not just our final moments,
in pursuit of our creations,
our counter-expressions of finality,
our catafalque of immortality projects?

I see that the squirrel has now gone,
and, with a flourish of poetry,
so beloved of these creatures,
I welcome her into my notebook.

DEATH WRITES

Death tries his hand at poetry.
'I'm innovating an interdimensional sestina,'
he explains.
'How's that working out for you?' I ask.
'It's not as easy as it sounds,' he replies.
'It doesn't sound easy at all,' I say.
'Exactly,' says Death.
'It's strange,' he continues,
'getting into the creative flow;
it's never really been my forte.'
'You don't say,' I say.
Death screws up the umpteenth page,
throws it against the wall,
and strikes a pose of poetic angst.
'Maybe you should start with something
a little simpler,' I suggest, 'like a limerick?'
Inspiration strikes Death,
and after a couple of minutes of fevered scribbling
he strikes a pose of poetic declamation.
And then he declaims:
'There once was a rider called Death,
Who looked, all the time, just like Death.
    "I wonder if Death
    Can die a good death?"
Said that black-hooded rider called Death.'
The declamation is, apparently, over.
'I feel so fulfilled!' exclaims Death, joyfully.
'Is this how it feels when you win a slam?' he asks.
'We write the poems we need to write,
or want to read,
or possibly the other way round,' I say,
hopefully avoiding the answer to his question
(no).
'Now can I try my interdimensional sestina?'
he asks.
'How about trying to get to grips
with blank verse first?' I suggest.

'I'm all ears,' says Death,
'*metaphorically speaking*, as we poets say.'
Forty-three minutes and seven seconds
into my explanation,
Death throws a tantrum.
'This is just stupid,' he huffs.
'That's a very modern reaction to blank verse,' I say.
'Perhaps you'd be more comfortable with free verse instead?'
'Which is...?' he asks.
I explain free verse to Death.
'Sounds like prose
masquerading as poetry,' he says.
'Every poem is poetry masquerading as poetry,'
I explain.
'Like the one you're writing now? No offence,'
he says.
'None taken,' I reply, as I tend to agree with him.
'It's what happens when you read
too much Kirill Medvedev, I think.'
'I'm bored with poetry,' says Death.
'I'm going to write a novel instead.
Where should I start?' he asks.
'At the end?' I say, having no idea
how one goes about writing a novel.
'Oh, yes, that sounds like an excellent idea,'
says Death.
'I can cope with endings.'
Having decided to start with an ending,
Death writes a novel consisting exclusively of endings.
One ending after another after another after another.
Death writes an abstract for his novel,
which he hopes will end up as a suitably inviting blurb:
'In his debut novel, *The Endings*, Death draws on his considerable experience as Death to write a fascinating literary collage of endings. Prescient, disturbing, honest, and underpinned with a sense of finality rarely experienced by the living, these endings encapsulate what it is to reach the end of a journey. This is a novel where "The End" is just the beginning, and one of them may even be yours.'

ICE CREAM

I find myself in a death mood.
Earlier in the day, I walked the hills.
Even at the height of summer, I think of Death,
I paused to write.
Death finds a place to sit, and opens up
his notebook, sketching everything he sees:
the skeleton of every living thing.
Even the clouds have skeletons for Death.
But, although I had wanted to write another poem about Death,
the lines did not look right upon the page.
It wasn't Death who was opening up his notebook
and sketching all those unseen skeletons;
it was me, sitting on an old wooden bench
(dedicated, as always, to a person – dead),
and it wasn't sketches I was drawing,
but cul-de-sac lines I was writing.
Perhaps blue sky and riots of green
do not provide the best backdrop for thought of Death.
Now, though, with a black sky to match my thoughts,
now seems the right time to meet Death on the page
once again.
It is just past midnight, and the day is dead;
it has become a yesterday.
The blue-white sky with its bright, shining sun;
the meadows on the hills;
the polite hellos to other walkers;
the footsteps taken; the thoughts thought –
everything about the day:
all gathered up into the arms of Death.
The day has passed away.

Death taps the inside of my skull.
'Well, this is awkward,' I say.
'I've just turned the light out.'
Death wants me to write about him again.
'But why should I write about you?' I ask.
'Why shouldn't I write *Ten Poems about Ice Cream* instead?'

I know the answer to this:
when you're writing about Death,
everyone knows what you mean.
Mention Death, and people find themselves
in the realm of the profound.
Ten Poems about Ice Cream
wouldn't be quite as attention-grabbing.
Who cares enough about ice cream
to read a sequence of poems about it?
Death, though, connects us all:
our secret fear, our eternal worry.
We avoid thinking about Death;
its reminders are unpleasant to contemplate.
Death: the final insult of existence, the terrible fate,
the appalling catastrophe, the unspeakable horror,
the annihilation of being and memory.
The End of Us.
None of this applies to ice cream.

MOJO

Death has been binge-watching a show on Netflix.
'It's called *How to Catch a Killer,*' he explains.
'I thought I might pick up some handy tips!'
I express surprise, having thought that
Death was beyond judgement
and was simply there to do a job.
'And also,' I say, 'surely you know who all the killers are,
what with being present at every murder?'
There's a bit of a silence,
belonging in the 'awkward' section of the Venn diagram.
'Y-y-y-e-e-e-e-e-s...' says Death,
as if trying to frame a suitable response.
This is unusual; Death is normally far more direct
in his communications.
He sighs a heavy sigh.
'Okay. Look, it was an attempt at a joke.
Really, I just wanted to see how incompetent the police were.
Unsurprisingly, if you're interested.'
I ask him how he found the show.
'It was quite interesting, up to a point.
I mean, I already knew who the killers were, obviously.
But, man – some of the procedures!
All that burden of proof, for a start.
Some people just look like killers, right?'
I explain that you can't just lock someone up
'because they look guilty'.
'Why not?' asks Death.
'If you look into a man's soul,
you can see the full burden of his sins.
The eyes being windows to the soul,
all you have to do is look into a man's eyes
to see if he's guilty or not.
Et voila! Case closed.'
I put it to Death that he could become an expert witness
in cases of murder.
'No, you see, that wouldn't work because...
Oh, shit. That's a joke, right?

Like a "Hey, Death! They should put you in charge
of the Cold Cases Unit.
You'd have a one hundred percent clear-up rate
and the unit could be disbanded in a matter of hours"
type thing.'
'Actually, that's not a bad idea,' I say.
'Really?' says Death, excitedly.
'Do you think... Oh, no, wait.
You're taking the piss again, aren't you?'
I apologise for my teasing.
And then it occurs to me
that maybe the Netflix cry for help was Death trying to find an escape:
an escape from the nature of his job;
an escape from being the ultimate and timeless
expert witness to all of the carnage,
bloodshed, war, barbarity,
injustice and unfairness; the ugliness;
the relentless horror of the end of existence
which has too often accompanied his appointed task.
'You're suffering from a very human predicament,' I suggest.
'You feel trapped in an endless cycle.
You have to do a job in order to justify your existence,
but you have started to doubt the job you have
and your ability to do it until retirement.
You feel that there is no escape,
and, like many people experiencing despair,
you're trying to divert your gaze,
if only for a few brief moments,
by watching sensationalist TV
with questionable production values.
Only problem is, you've unconsciously chosen a show
which is related to the cause of your angst,
like a doctor watching *Casualty*,
or a teacher watching *Big Schoo*l,
or a dentist watching *Question Time*,
which, admittedly, isn't a show but more of a shower of shit,'

I conclude.
I put to Death that he watch something
completely unrelated to his occupation,
or his general mode of existence,
and leave him to it.
Half an hour later,
I walk into the room to see
Death's Netflix page on the screen.
Continue watching for Death, it reads,
and I see *Friends*, the red line indicating
that he's a few minutes into episode one.
A text appears on my phone.
Guess what? it starts. *I got my mojo back!*
Thanks! D xx

WALK INTO THE SEA

Working on the theory
that everything is a metaphor for something,
I decide to write a poem about the sea.

I can hear it now, behind me,
the idle rise and fall of the Mediterranean waves:
waves, which, it seems to me,
aren't really trying hard enough;
waves which can't be bothered.

The sea. I feel it ought only to get a passing mention
in the somewhere else of a different poem,
rather than a whole poem to itself.

After all, what does it care?
Oblivious to its salt, its water,
the fish, the sand, the boats, the plastic,
even the sky which reflects off its unstill surface.

'Another poem about me?' it will not say.
'Oh, how terrifically original.'

Maybe the sea is better used as a question mark,
or a little splash of colour;
maybe a *blink and you miss it* hint of menace,
or perhaps the suggestion of summer,
depending on the poem it crops up in.

But an entire poem?

While you were reading this, I've been thinking:
what exactly is the sea a metaphor for here,
in this particular poem?
Answer me that.

While you formulate your answer,
I shall turn to face the sea and walk towards it,
anticipating the enjoyment of the water
washing the sun off my skin,
before I return, cooled enough to finish this poem.

And as I walk into the sea,
I will think about the story of my father,
into a second bottle of whisky,

staggering into Dublin's bay at some ungodly hour,
willing the waves to take him,
not quite yet fully resolved
to end it all.

DANCE

I wander among the trees in search of life.
The sky is no longer overhead,
but in my heart, where it beats in time
to my ceaseless anxiety.
The leaves don't fall; they detach themselves,
then meander earthwards in a dance with gravity.
Is this why trees exist?
So that leaves can dance with gravity?
We think of dances beginning on floors,
but a floor is where the leaf dance ends.
The merging with earth begins.
Rain, wind, time:
and the leaf becomes the floor.
How long before its atoms emerge,
as flower, grass, air, or even sap?
It all goes on without us noticing.
The next time you see a leaf, though.
Your branches twist around my words
till branch and word are one,
waiting for blossom.
The atoms are always dancing.
Can you feel them? Is that what breathing is?
Is that what living is?
Our eternal atoms continue after
what is to become of us?
has been answered.
We cannot be left behind, not fully.
You were born into this world.
No, you were born out of this world,
and once born you remain, forever, somewhere.
After my breathing has stopped,
I will wander among the trees again,
my heart will return to the sky,
and perhaps I shall dance with the leaves.

ACKNOWLEDGEMENTS:

Many thanks to: Maggie Doyle, Spoz, Brenda Read-Brown, Clive Birnie, Bridget Hart, Harriet Evans, Rupert Heale, James Green, Fintan, Conor, Declan, Myles, Aidan, and Gemma.

Picture of trees by Edna Clarke-Hall (1879-1979).

Lightning Source UK Ltd.
Milton Keynes UK
UKHW021828141120
373369UK00006B/55

9 781911 570998